WITHDRAWN

D1735997

Exploring World Cultures

Sweden

Joanne Mattern

Cavendish Square
New York

Published in 2018 by Cavendish Square Publishing, LLC
243 5th Avenue, Suite 136, New York, NY 10016

Copyright © 2018 by Cavendish Square Publishing, LLC

First Edition

No part of this publication may be reproduced, stored in a retrieval system, or transmitted in any form or by any means—electronic, mechanical, photocopying, recording, or otherwise—without the prior permission of the copyright owner. Request for permission should be addressed to Permissions, Cavendish Square Publishing, 243 5th Avenue, Suite 136, New York, NY 10016. Tel (877) 980-4450; fax (877) 980-4454.

Website: cavendishsq.com

This publication represents the opinions and views of the author based on his or her personal experience, knowledge, and research. The information in this book serves as a general guide only. The author and publisher have used their best efforts in preparing this book and disclaim liability rising directly or indirectly from the use and application of this book.

All websites were available and accurate when this book was sent to press.

Library of Congress Cataloging-in-Publication Data

Names: Mattern, Joanne, 1963- author.
Title: Sweden / Joanne Mattern.
Description: New York : Cavendish Square Publishing, [2018] | Series: Exploring world cultures | Includes index.
Identifiers: LCCN 2017016351 (print) | LCCN 2017016506 (ebook) | ISBN 9781502630278 (pbk.) | ISBN 9781502630292 (library bound) | ISBN 9781502630285 (6 pack) | ISBN 9781502630308 (E-book)
Subjects: LCSH: Sweden--Juvenile literature.
Classification: LCC DL609 (ebook) | LCC DL609 .M28 2018 (print) | DDC 948.5--dc23
LC record available at https://lccn.loc.gov/2017016351

Editorial Director: David McNamara
Editor: Kristen Susienka
Copy Editor: Alex Tessman
Associate Art Director: Amy Greenan
Designer: Graham Abbott
Production Coordinator: Karol Szymczuk
Photo Research: J8 Media

The photographs in this book are used by permission and through the courtesy of: Cover Maskot/Getty Images; p. 5 Marie Linner/Shtterstock.com; p. 6 Bergserg/DigitalVision/Getty Images; p. 7 Christian Aslund/Lonely Planet Images/Getty Images; p. 8 Matt de Lange/Shutterstock.com; p. 9 Private Collection/The Stapleton Collection/Bridgeman Images; p. 10 AFP/Getty Images; p. 11 Krzyzak/Shutterstock.com; p. 12 Bloomberg/Getty Images; p. 13 Ingunn B. Haslekas/Moment Mobile/Getty Images; p. 14 Erlend Haarberg/National Geographic/Getty Images; p. 15 Jrgen Larsson/age fotostock/Getty Images; p. 16 Christian Science Monitor/Getty Images; p. 18 Juliana Wiklund/Johner Images/Getty Images; p. 19 Tomasz Wozniak/Shutterstock.com; p. 20 a40757/Shuterstock.com; p. 21 Mikhail Markovskiy/Shuterstock.com; p. 22 Jo Crebbin/Shutterstock.com; p. 24 Rolf 52/Shutterstock.com; p. 26 Ulf Huett Nilsson/Getty Images; p. 27 Christian Science Monitor/Getty Images; p. 28 AS Food Studio/Shutterstock.com; p. 29 Christer Fredriksson/Lonely Planet Images/Getty Images.

Printed in the United States of America

Contents

Introduction		4
Chapter 1	Geography	6
Chapter 2	History	8
Chapter 3	Government	10
Chapter 4	The Economy	12
Chapter 5	The Environment	14
Chapter 6	The People Today	16
Chapter 7	Lifestyle	18
Chapter 8	Religion	20
Chapter 9	Language	22
Chapter 10	Arts and Festivals	24
Chapter 11	Fun and Play	26
Chapter 12	Food	28
Glossary		30
Find Out More		31
Index and About the Author		32

Introduction

Sweden is a country in northern Europe. It is located on a piece of land called the Scandinavian **Peninsula**. Sweden shares this peninsula with another country called Norway.

Almost ten million people live in Sweden. Most people live in or near large cities, such as Stockholm or Malmö. Most people who live in this country are **ethnic** Swedes. However, Sweden is also home to many refugees from around the world.

Sweden is a land of forests and mountains. The country also has plains and valleys. There are many lakes and rivers in Sweden. Most of the nation has a mild climate, but winters in the north can be very cold.

People in Sweden work hard, but they also enjoy sports, games, and having fun. Swedes celebrate festivals and holidays. They share food with family and friends. Sweden is a country with many special traditions and an interesting history.

Sweden has cold, snowy winters. Many people enjoy winter sports, like ice skating, even in the coldest weather.

Geography

Sweden is a long, narrow country. Norway borders Sweden to the west. Finland borders Sweden on the north and east.

The Baltic Sea lies on Sweden's east and south. The Gulf of Bothnia lies to the northeast. The narrow Danish Straits separate Sweden from Denmark in the southwest. Sweden's southwestern coast lies on the Kattegat and the Skagerrak. These bodies of water connect to the North Sea.

This map shows Sweden and other countries on the Scandinavian Peninsula.

Northern Sweden has many high mountains, lakes, and rivers. The central part of Sweden has

The Midnight Sun

In Sweden, the sun never sets during part of the summer, and it does not rise during part of the winter.

hills, plains, forests, and river valleys. The far southern part has flat plains.

Most of Sweden has a mild climate. Summer temperatures are around 70 degrees Fahrenheit (21 degrees Celsius). Snow covers all parts of Sweden during the winter months.

A person walks through the snow on a gloomy winter day.

FACT!
About 15 percent of Sweden lies inside the Arctic Circle.

History

Thousands of years ago, Sweden was covered by ice. Over time, the ice melted. About twelve thousand years ago, the first people arrived.

Long ago, Vikings sailed around Europe in longboats like this one.

By 800 CE, the Vikings lived in Sweden. They sailed to other countries in Europe, attacking and stealing from other cultures. They also traded with Russia and other countries.

In 1000, Erik Jedvardsson (Erik IX) became king. However, local **provinces** still made their own laws. Later, the Folkung **dynasty** ruled the entire nation. In 1523, Gustav Vasa (Gustav I)

FACT!

Sweden once controlled Finland, Estonia, and parts of Germany.

became king. He made many changes to the Swedish government.

Sweden was neutral during World War I and World War II. After World War II, Sweden had a strong **economy**, which lasted until the 1990s. Later, the nation had economic problems, but it recovered. Sweden remains a strong country today.

A King and a Saint

King Erik IX later became a saint. He is the patron saint of Sweden.

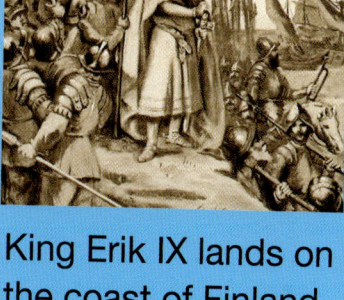

King Erik IX lands on the coast of Finland in 1157.

Government

Sweden is a constitutional monarchy. That means the nation has a king and queen, but they have no real power. Instead, a parliament called the Riksdag represents the Swedish people. People vote for members of parliament every four years.

Swedish prime minister Fredrik Reinfeldt (*right*) attends a Nordic Council meeting in Finland in 2012.

The prime minister is the head of the government. He or she is the leader of the

Sweden is divided into twenty-one counties. Each county is run by a governor and a council.

parliament. Parliament has 349 members. It makes laws, enforces taxes, plans the budget, and decides on how the country will work with other countries.

Sweden's **constitution** explains how the government works. It states that all power comes from the people. Everyone is equal. It also describes the freedoms people have, including freedom of worship and freedom of speech.

Capital City

Stockholm is the capital of Sweden. The city is built on fourteen islands connected by fifty-seven bridges.

Parliament's headquarters are in this grand building in Stockholm.

The Economy

Sweden has a strong economy. Most companies are privately owned, while others are owned by the government.

Many Swedes work in high-tech industrial jobs, such as this worker in a truck factory.

The nation has a large iron and steel industry. Sweden makes tools, airplanes, cars, ships, machinery, and electronics.

Forestry is also important. Swedish wood is made into furniture. Its lumber is sent all around the world.

Farming and fishing are a big part of the Swedish economy. Farmers raise livestock such as dairy cows. They also grow many crops, including cereal, potatoes, wheat, oats, and vegetables.

Most of Sweden's goods are sent to other countries.

Many Swedes work in service industries. They are government workers, teachers, bankers, scientists, storeowners, and restaurant staff. Many Swedes also work in transportation.

Money Matters

Swedish money is called kronor. Sweden uses both coins and paper money. Paper money comes in different colors. The front has a picture of a famous Swede. The back has a picture from Swedish history or nature.

This basket holds many Swedish kronor, both bills and coins.

The Environment

Because Sweden has such a long coastline and so many lakes, many fish and birds live in the country. The lakes are filled with salmon and other fish.

Oil covers the surface of a polluted lake in Sweden.

Many different mammals and birds live in Sweden's thick forests. The largest is the moose. Deer, wolves, lynx, and boars also live in the forests.

The arctic fox is one of the few animals that lives above the Arctic Circle. It is endangered in Sweden. Climate change has made the cold area warmer, so animals like the

FACT!
More than two thousand otters live in Sweden's rivers and coastal waters.

red fox, which is much larger than the arctic fox, can now live above the Arctic Circle and eat the arctic fox's food.

Industries are important to Sweden's economy, but they also pollute the nation's water and land. The government is trying to reduce the amount of pollution and protect nature.

A gray seal appears to wave as it swims in a Swedish lake.

The Baltic Gray Seal

Sweden and other countries are working to protect the Baltic gray seal. It lives in the Baltic Sea.

The People Today

Ethnic Swedes usually have blond hair and fair skin. They are descended from the ancient German tribes that came to Scandinavia thousands of years ago. However, today, immigrants from all over the world have come to live in Sweden. More than one-quarter of the nation's people are immigrants or have a parent who is an immigrant.

This Indian family moved to Sweden for better job opportunities.

Immigrants have been coming to Sweden since World War II. Today, many refugees travel there from the Middle

East. They are escaping war and violence. The Swedish government is working to help immigrants fit into Swedish society.

FACT!

Between 1850 and 1930, more than one million people left Sweden because of the poor economy.

A Traditional Culture

The Samis are a minority people who live in the polar area. They probably came from Russia thousands of years ago. Samis used to be **nomads** who raised reindeer for a living. Today, most Samis live in one place all year.

Lifestyle

The Swedish government helps its people. It provides them with free health care and free education. Swedes pay some of the highest taxes in the world. In return, they receive these services.

Swedish families value the time they spend together.

Sweden tries to treat everyone equally. Most people have the same standard of living. Men and women have equal rights. Sweden has one of the highest rates of working women in the world.

Family life is important to Swedes. However, the nation has a low marriage rate. Many couples

FACT!
Uppsala University was founded in 1477. It is Sweden's oldest university.

live together and have children even though they are not married.

About 85 percent of Swedes live in the city. Many people own homes in the country and enjoy spending vacations there.

Going to School

Swedish children start school at age six or seven. About one-third of students go on to college after finishing senior high school.

University Hall is the main building at Uppsala University.

Religion

There is no official religion in Sweden, but Christianity has been popular since the 1000s. The Roman Catholic Church was the main religion until 1526. That year, King Gustav I created the Church of Sweden. It is a part of the Lutheran faith. Today, the church and government are separate. People can choose to belong to the Church of Sweden or not.

This Swedish church shows a traditional building style.

FACT!

Until 1996, any child born to a member of the Church of Sweden was automatically a member too.

Many immigrants brought their own religions to Sweden. Today, Muslims make up Sweden's second-largest religious group. Sweden also has a small population of Eastern Orthodox Christians, Roman Catholics, and members of other Christian churches. There are also Jews, Mormons, Buddhists, and Hindus. About one-quarter of Swedes do not practice any religion.

Norse Religion

Before Christianity came to Sweden, people followed the Norse religion. They worshipped many gods, including Thor and Odin.

Sweden still honors its ancient gods. This statue in Stockholm shows the famous Norse god Thor.

21

Language

The Swedish language is part of the North Germanic family of languages. Swedish sounds a lot like Danish, Norwegian, and Icelandic. That is because they are all related.

These street signs show Swedish place names in the traditional alphabet.

English is also a Germanic language. Many words in Swedish are similar to English words. For example, *bok* means "book" and *moder* means "mother."

FACT!

Children learn both Swedish and English in school. They start learning English around age eight or nine.

The Swedish Alphabet

The Swedish alphabet has twenty-nine letters. Twenty-six of them are the same as the English alphabet. The other three letters are *å, ä,* and *ö.*

The Swedish government recognizes five minority languages. They are Finnish, Sami, Romani, Yiddish, and Meänkieli. Preserving these native languages helps preserve different cultures.

Sweden's many immigrants have brought their own languages to the nation. Today, it is not unusual to hear people speaking Arabic or African languages.

Arts and Festivals

Swedes enjoy art, music, dance, and literature. Folk dancers often perform at festivals. They wear traditional clothing and dance to music played on the fiddle and the key harp. Pop and rock music are also very popular in Sweden.

Musicians play traditional instruments at a Swedish folk music festival.

Sweden is also known for its literature. August Strindberg is one of Sweden's greatest writers. Strindberg wrote plays and novels. Astrid Lindgren is another popular Swedish author. She created the famous children's character Pippi Longstocking.

FACT!

Sweden's first works of art were carved into rocks more than four thousand years ago.

Swedes have created beautiful art. The nation also produces beautifully designed cookware, pottery, glassworks, and furniture. Sweden has also given the world famous movie actors, actresses, and directors.

Saint Lucia's Day

Swedes celebrate Saint Lucia's Day on December 13. A girl wears a lighted crown and a white robe as she leads a procession of girls and boys.

Fun and Play

Swedes like to stay active. Popular sports include soccer, tennis, and golf. Winter sports like skiing, ice hockey, and skating are also popular. During the spring and summer, Swedes like to enjoy the outdoors. They go hiking, ride bikes, and spend time in the nation's many parks and natural areas.

A mother helps her daughter ski on one of Sweden's many ski slopes.

FACT!

Zlatan Ibrahimović is one of Sweden's biggest sports stars. He became the captain of the national soccer team in 2010.

Water sports are also popular. Many Swedes enjoy swimming, boating, and fishing on the nation's lakes or along its coastline.

Swedes who live in the city enjoy shopping and eating out. They enjoy getting together with friends and family over a good meal.

Swedes also enjoy quiet time at home. Swedish families often spend Friday nights watching a movie or playing games together.

A family enjoys a picnic in a Stockholm park.

Long Vacations

Swedes have lots of time to enjoy themselves. Most workers have six to ten weeks of vacation a year.

Food

Meat is an important part of Swedish meals. Swedes enjoy pork and beef. Northern families eat reindeer meat. Swedish meatballs are a popular dish in Sweden and around the world.

This traditional meal includes Swedish meatballs in lingonberry sauce, served with potatoes.

Swedes also eat a lot of fish. Fish is eaten fresh, but it is also pickled, cured, or salted. These practices preserve the fish so it can be eaten all year round.

Milk and coffee are popular Swedish drinks.

Because Sweden has a short growing season, fresh vegetables are not an important part of the diet. However, root vegetables such as turnips and beets are common. Swedes also enjoy potatoes. Berries are the most popular fruit.

This smörgåsbord includes many different meats, vegetables, and fruits.

A Smörgåsbord of Food

A smörgåsbord is a traditional Swedish meal. Many different hot and cold dishes are put out. Diners help themselves to whatever food they like. Dishes include fish, cheese, cold meat, Swedish meatballs, cakes, pies, and fruit.

Glossary

constitution   A document that describes the laws of a country.

dynasty   A series of rulers belonging to the same family.

economy   A system of goods or services that helps make a country successful.

ethnic   Related to people who have a common national or cultural tradition.

nomads   People who wander around instead of living in one place.

peninsula   Land that is surrounded by water on three sides.

provinces   Districts in a country.

Find Out More

Books

Koestler-Grack, Rachel A. *Sweden*. Minneapolis, MN: Bellwether Media, 2010.

Murray, Julie. *Sweden*. Minneapolis, MN: Big Buddy Books, 2015.

Website

Geography for Kids: Sweden

http://www.ducksters.com/geography/country/sweden.php

Video

Sweden: Twelve Interesting Facts About Sweden

https://www.youtube.com/watch?v=1krRNPF7nhk

This video includes fun facts about Swedish history, culture, and food.

Index

constitution, 10–11

dynasty, 8

economy, 9, 12, 15, 17

ethnic, 4, 16

family, 5, 16, 18, 18, 22, 27–28, 27

fish, 12, 14, 27–29

lakes, 4, 6, 14, 27

nomads, 17

peninsula, 4, 6

provinces, 8

winter, 4–5, 7, 7, 26

About the Author

Joanne Mattern is the author of more than 250 books for children. She specializes in writing nonfiction and has explored many different places in her writing. Her favorite topics include history, travel, sports, biography, and animals. Mattern lives in New York State with her husband, four children, and several pets.

31901062502846